Listen Around
Teacher's Book

Geoffrey Winters and Jim Northfield

Contents

[Pages 3–40]   Background notes and answer for teachers

[Pages 1–8]   Centre pull-out section comprising 8 students' copymaster worksheets.

A Student's Book and a cassette accompany this book
Other titles in the GCSE Music Skills series
Listen, Compose, Perform *by Geoffrey Winters*
Composing *by Martin Hinckley*

Longman Group UK Limited,
Longman House, Burnt Mill, Harlow,
Essex CM20 2JE, England
and Associated Companies throughout the world.

First published 1990
Second impression 1990
Set in 10/12 point Palatino (Linotron 202)
Produced by Longman Group (FE) Limited
Printed in Hong Kong

ISBN 0 582 01341 0

Acknowledgements

We are grateful to the following for permission to
reproduce music copyright material:
Boosey & Hawkes Ltd/Edition Musica Budapest for
melodic outline of Bartók's 'The Highway Robber'
from *For Children* Vol. II, No. 31 © 1946 by Boosey &
Hawkes Inc.; English Folk Dance & Song Society for
tunes to 'Dorest four-hand reel', 'The old grey cat',
'Gilderoy' and 'My love she's but a Lassie yet', tune
& words to 'Blow the Man Down, Bullies' from
Community Dances Manuals © EDFSS; International
Music Publications for eight bars rhythm from
'Sweet Adeline' by Harry Armstrong & Richard
Gerard © 1903 M. Witmark & Sons USA. Sub-pubd
by B. Feldman & Co. Ltd, London WC2H OLD.
Reproduced by permission of EMI Music Pubg Ltd
& IMP; Oxford University Press for tune to 'Wata
come a me y'eye' from *Folk Songs of Jamaica* collected
by Tom Murray © 1952; R. Smith & Co. Ltd,
Watford, England for melodic excerpts from
Bandutopia by R. Farnon & 'On the trail' from *The*
Golden West by S. Johnson; Universal Edition
(London) Ltd for bars 5–12-trombone part from
Kodály *Háry János* fourth movement.

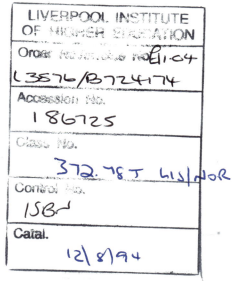

Introduction

Listen Around is a graded listening course which complements the Listening section of *Listen, Compose, Perform* in a number of ways. One of these is that it widens the range of style presented by adding to the largely orchestral repertoire of the core book, examples of folk, rock and jazz, electronic and synthesised techniques, music for brass band, and vocal and instrumental ensemble music from the 16th to 20th century. In addition, *Listen Around* offers some easier exercises which will allow a more gradual incline towards the GCSE listening tests than would be possible with the core book alone.

Listen Around takes the basic elements of music and treats them under the headings **Beats and bars, Shapes and sizes, Chords and cadences, Groups and families** and **Light and shade.** Each of these five sections is repeated at four levels and at each level there are two Listening tests A and B.

Listen Around does not purport to be a theory book and theoretical explanations are rarely given. However, a glance at the panels headed **Featured elements** will show where such explanation may be necessary, either before or after the listening experience. Although it addresses many of the problems associated with systematic aural training, *Listen Around*, as its name implies, ranges wider in trying to develop an overall awareness and feel for the music encountered.

The majority of exercises are accompanied by a recording and only a few rely on the aural recall of well-known tunes like *The First Nowell*. In some circumstances it may be necessary to play these tunes so that memories are refreshed or cultural backgrounds accommodated. Most examples have been specially recorded for this book and the instruction given to the performers was to record at 'as moderate a tempo as possible consistent with style and mood.' An example may be played by the teacher at a slower tempo with the aid of the notation in this book.

Many children find the relationship of sound to sign and vice versa difficult. Within the diversity presented the practical limitations of tape time preclude a multiplicity of exercises in any one area. It is therefore desirable, if not essential, for teachers to supplement these with additional material. Such material will offer opportunities to draw on ethno-centric as well as traditional and popular cultural sources. The individual teacher is uniquely placed to understand and reflect the students' needs in a way that no general overview can encompass. Towards this end a number of suggestions are offered for each section under the heading **Related listening** and these may be used both for specific aural development and for the equally important general widening of musical understanding. The selection is by no means exhaustive as a deliberate effort has been made, particularly with respect to rock and pop, to limit the references to reasonably

accessible material wherever possible. Some albums and works, like *Sergeant Pepper* and *Háry János*, are referred to more than once both for musical and practical purposes. Where examples are not readily available from library sources, they may well be forthcoming from pupils and colleagues.

The solutions to a good number of exercises depend in part on the ability to recognize the repetition of a motif or phrase which appears elsewhere in an exact or similar form. The appreciation of such recurrence is not only a help in arriving at the correct answer, but is also crucial in the understanding of structure, and in the response to the rhetoric of the music itself. These points apply equally to composing, performing and listening. Awareness of the interaction between all three should be constantly encouraged.

Listening to pop music

For many teachers the use of pop music as a listening experience in the classroom has been a bone of contention. To the student it is often seen as no more than an attempt to inject a fashionable element into listening periods which, at worst, can degenerate into a totally indiscriminate desert-island-disc-type session with the unfortunate teacher marooned on the shifting sands of style, fashion and hero worship.

The enjoyment and appreciation of pop music is by no means the prerogative of the adolescent, but, to return to the analogy, to chart a course through the unmarked seas of the current pop scene is as dangerous as it is futile because so much of what is currently 'in' is rooted in a peer group culture, whose survival depends upon providing alternatives to any system which seeks to embrace it.

Pop music often appears to be little more than a media-manipulating commercial enterprise, but whilst its validity as an art form would undoubtedly provoke discussion far beyond the bounds of these pages, we suggest that popular music could certainly be considered a craft that requires discerning musical decisions to be made. The resultant diversity of styles and techniques found within the confines of the simple structure of a three-minute pop song can provide valid listening material from simple rhythmic and harmonic structures to questions of timbre, synthesis and sound production techniques. The latter are dealt with simply in the level 4 **Light and shade** section of the student's book.

It should be possible for the pupils to find many good examples of a lot of the theoretical ground covered in *Listen Around* within their own record or tape collections. This road to a more critical analytical ear should be encouraged. The value judgements involved in the assessment of pop, and the question of what constitutes good and bad music will never be addressed without listening to what is actually there.

Level 1

Beats and bars 1

Featured elements		
1	$\frac{2}{4}$	♩ ♫ 𝄽 −
2	$\frac{3}{4}$	
3	$\frac{4}{4}$	−
4–5		♩. ♪

Recordings	
1–4	Drum-kit rhythms (×2)

Answers

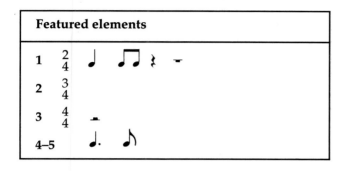

1   snare drum
    bass drum

2   3 beats in a bar

    Rhythm in third bar is second example

3   cymbal
    side drum
    bass drum

4   (a)
    (b)
    (c)

Related listening

'Reprise' from *Sergeant Pepper's Lonely Hearts Club Band:* The Beatles (for ♩ 𝄾 ♫ 𝄾 on drum kit)
Stravinsky: *Petrushka,* 'Merrymakers' music' from 1st tableau (for ♩ ♫)
'March of the Siamese Children' from *The King and I:* Rodgers and Hammerstein (for ♩ ♫♩ ♫)
'Superstition' from *Talking Book:* Stevie Wonder (for basic drum pulse with overlaid rhythms)
Smetana: *The Bartered Bride,* Act 1, first chorus (for ♩. ♪ and stepwise melody)
Tchaikovsky: Piano Concerto no. 1, 1st movement, main theme (for ♩. ♪ in triple time)

Shapes and sizes 1

Featured elements
1 Stepwise melody
2 Occasional jumps
3 Repeated notes
4 Stepwise shapes
5 Steps, jumps and repeated notes

Recordings
1 Melodic fragments (×2)
2 No recording
3(a) German country dance (×2)
(b) Purcell: *Musick's handmaid*, 'Rigadon' (×2)
(c) Bulgarian folk dance (×2)
4 *Oh the praties they grow small*, Irish folk song
5 No recording

Answers

1 (a)  (b)  (c)

2 Adding lines in front of words with melodic jumps

The first Nowell the angel did say
Was to certain poor shepherds in fields │ as they lay;

My │ grandfather's clock was too tall for the │ shelf │
So it stood ninety years on the floor.

3 (a) German country dance

(b) Purcell: Rigadon

(c) Bulgarian folk dance

4 Oh the praties they grow small
Over here, over here;
Oh the praties they grow small and we dig them in the fall,
And we eat them skins and all,
Over here, over here.

Notice than in keeping with this carol's dance origins it has been notated in $\frac{2}{4}$ time rather than in the traditional, but rather ponderous, $\frac{4}{4}$ time. You may wish to discuss this with the pupils.

Related listening

Brahms: *Academic Festival Overture*, 'student song' (for stepwise and repeated notes)
Prokofiev: 'Classical' Symphony, fourth movement, 2nd subject (for repeated notes)
Mozart: *The Marriage of Figaro*, overture (for stepwise patterns, scales and some repeated notes)
Saint-Saëns: *Carnival of the Animals*, finale (for repeated notes)
'The Surrey with the Fringe on Top' from *Oklahoma* (for repeated notes)
'Getting Better' from *Sergeant Pepper's Lonely Hearts Club Band:* The Beatles (for repeated notes in inverted pedal and for octave movement in bass)

Chords and cadences 1

Featured elements

1–2	Drones
3	Identification of perfect 5ths and octaves
4(a)	2- and 4-bar phrases
(b)	longer phrases
(c)	3-bar phrases
5	Solo/chorus textures
6	Recognition of: octave doubling harmonised bars

Recordings

1	Bulgarian folk dance in three presentations
2	Examples of drones on guitar, harpsichord, bagpipe and tabla
3	Synthesised intervals
4(a)	François Couperin: *Les Fastes de la grande et ancienne Mxnxstrxndxsx*, Buffoons, jugglers and rope dancers with bears and monkeys
(b)	No recording
(c)	Bulgarian folk dance
5	*Sweet Adeline* (8 bar extract)
6	Mozart: theme from Variations on *Unser dummer Pöbel meint* K 455.

Answers

1 (a) high and shrill
(b) sweetly, with an extra part
(c) with long, low held sounds

Chords and cadences 1

2 First example is c (on a guitar)
   Second example is d (on a harpsichord)
   Third example is a (on bagpipes)
   Fourth example is b (on tabla with sitar)

3 (a) Intervals 2 and 5 were perfect 5ths
   (b) Intervals 3 and 4 were octaves

4 (a) Couperin

4	4	4	4
2	2	4	
2	2	4	

   (b) Good King Wenceslas

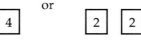
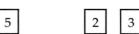

4		2	2
4	or	2	2
4		2	2
5		2	3

   (c) Bulgarian folk dance

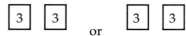

3	3	or	3	3
6			3	3

5

Sweet Adeline

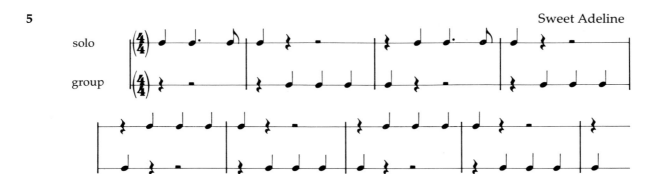

solo

group

6 Mozart: *Variations* K 455
   1   2   ③   ④   5   6   ⑦   ⑧
   ⑨ ⑩ ⑪ ⑫ 13 14 ⑮ ⑯

Related listening

'Within you, without you' from *Sergeant Pepper's Lonely Hearts Club Band:* The Beatles (for drone on tabla and sitar)
Try also to listen to other Indian music with examples of drones.
'Galtee Farmer' from *Commoner's Crown:* Steeleye Span (for decorated drone)
Shostakovitch: String Quartet no. 8, second movement (for arpeggiated drone which is later inverted); fourth movement (for a long held pedal note)
Menotti: *Amahl and the Night Visitors,* pipe music as curtain rises (for drone with ♩. ♪ rhythm in bass)
Schubert: *Die Winterreise,* 'The Organ Grinder' (for drone and textural contrast)
African singing, sea shanties and American Negro music (for call and response techniques in which a solo singer is answered by a group in unison or near unison)
Sousa: *The Washington Post* march (for textural contrast and for antiphonal treatment)
Beethoven: Piano Concerto no.4, 2nd movement (for octaves contrasted with chords)

Groups and families 1

Featured elements
1 Keyboard instruments
2 Guitars
3 Drum kit percussion
4 Latin-American percussion
5 Recorder consort
6 Recognition of some of above

Recordings
1 Piano, organ, synthesiser, harpsichord
2 Classical guitar, folk guitar, electric guitar
3 Drum kit percussion
4 Latin-American percussion
5 Recorder consort
6 Instrumental pairs

Answers

1 Harpsichord and piano

2 Classical guitar   (mellow)
    Folk guitar   (metallic)
    Electric guitar   (distorted)

3 Illustrative only

4 Whistle plays additional part in Latin-American example

5 A recorder consort resembles the sound of an organ, for both produce their sound with pipes.

6 (a) Drum kit and electric guitar
     (b) Recorder and harpsichord
     (c) Latin-American percussion and
           synthesiser

Related listening

Tchaikovsky: *Nutcracker Suite*, 'Sugar Plum Fairy' (for celesta)
Saint-Saëns: *Carnival of the Animals*, 'Aquarium' (for two pianos)
Bartók: Sonata for Two Pianos and Percussion, second movement (for drums, cymbals, xylophone and tam-tam and piano sound with contrasted textures)
In addition, any extended illustration of other keyboard and fretted instruments (including banjo and lute) and also recorders.

Light and shade 1

Featured elements		Recordings	
1	*forte* and *piano*	**1–5**	Rhythmic patterns with dynamic variation (×2)
2–4	*crescendo* and *diminuendo*		
5	accents		

Answers

1   f p f p

$f \longrightarrow p\ (<)\, f$

2 (a)

(b)

(c)

3

4   bar 7 has a *crescendo*

5

Related listening

Baroque music (where repeats may be played *forte* or *piano* or with different registrations on harpsichord or organ)

Haydn: Symphony no. 94 'The Surprise', second movement (for sudden *forte*)

'If leaving me is easy' from *Face Value*: Phil Collins (for sudden *forte* towards end of track)

Shostakovitch: String Quartet no.8, fourth movement (for sudden *fortes* in *pp* surroundings)

Beethoven: Sonata in C minor, op.13 *Pathétique*, first movement (for dynamic contrasts in slow introduction and then *crescendos* over pedal points)

Holst: *The Planets*, 'Mars' (for long *crescendo*)

Ravel: *Bolero* (for even longer *crescendo*)

Tubular Bells: Mike Oldfield (for sudden *sforzando* chord in opening A minor melody)

Beethoven: *Prometheus* Overture (for dynamic contrasts in slow introduction, for stepwise shapes in *Allegro* 1st subject, for *sf* accents and then for chord tunes in 2nd subject (see Levels 2 and 3)

Listening test 1A

Béla Bartók: 'The Highway Robber'
no.31 from *For Children* vol. 2

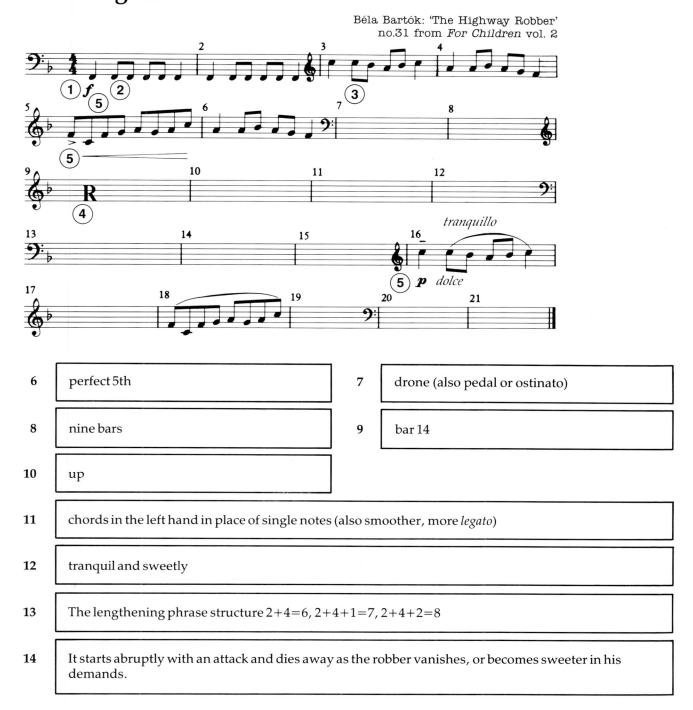

| 6 | perfect 5th | 7 | drone (also pedal or ostinato) |

| 8 | nine bars | 9 | bar 14 |

| 10 | up |

| 11 | chords in the left hand in place of single notes (also smoother, more *legato*) |

| 12 | tranquil and sweetly |

| 13 | The lengthening phrase structure 2+4=6, 2+4+1=7, 2+4+2=8 |

| 14 | It starts abruptly with an attack and dies away as the robber vanishes, or becomes sweeter in his demands. |

Listening test 1B

The Marionette (J.N.)

9	a xylophone	10	repeated a tone lower

11	a b (c) d	12	(answer marked on music)

13	descending stepwise melody

14	Latin-American percussion

Level 2

Beats and bars 2

Featured elements	
1	𝅗𝅥 and 𝅝
2	¾ rhythmic patterns
3	𝄽 - - ♫♩
4	𝄾 on first part of beat
5–7	(triplet) ♫♩

Recordings	
1	German folk tune (×2)
2	Gospel style piano (×2)
3	Two-part melody (×2)
4	Reggae
5	Cowbell and bass drum (×2)
6	Snare drum military rhythm (×2)
7	Mendelssohn: *A Midsummer Night's Dream*, Wedding March (extract)

Answers

1

2 bar 3 (b) /

bar 7 (c) /

3

4 There are three rhythmic clusters in reggae example.

5 Cowbell

Bass Drum

6

7 Mendelssohn: *A Midsummer Night's Dream*, Wedding March is likely to be heard at a wedding in a church.

Shapes and sizes 2

Shapes and sizes 2

Featured elements	Recordings
1 Recognition of: melodic steps melodic jumps **2–3** Octave jumps and other intervals **4** Phrase structures with open and closed endings, chord-note tunes	Examples of chord-note tunes from trumpet call, Mozart, and *In the mood* **1** Melodies of: Handel: *Arrival of the Queen of Sheba* (×2) Bach: *Brandenburg Concerto* no. 5 in D (×2) **2** No recording **3** *My Love She's but a Lassie Yet* Example of Jamaican folk-tune: *Linstead Market* **4(a)** *Wata come a me y'eye* (b) Dorset four-hand reel (c) *Jessie James*

Answers

1 Handel: (jumps steps)
  Bach: (jumps steps jumps)

2

3 The downward octave jump in *My Love she's but a Lassie Yet* occurs seven times. The fourth time it is from D to D.

Jamaican folk song: *Wata come a me y'eye*

Dorset four-hand reel

American Traditional: *Jessie James*

Related listening

Oxygène: Jean Michel Jarre (for chord-note tune with some steps)
Gilbert and Sullivan: *Iolanthe,* 'Entrance and March of the Peers' (for chord-note tune and ♩. ♪ in chorus entry)
Haydn: Symphony no. 94 in G, third movement (for jumping tune followed by stepwise shapes)
The Sailor's Hornpipe (for octave and other jumps)
Deep River (for octave jumps, ♩. ♪ and longer sounds from tied notes)
'All I ask' from *Phantom of the Opera:* Andrew Lloyd Webber (for swooping jumps up to a ninth)
Kodály: *Háry János,* 'Viennese Musical Clock' (for chord-note jumps and steps contrasted throughout and also open and closed endings in main tune)

Chords and cadences 2

Featured elements
1 Tonic and dominant chords Identification of perfect cadences juxtaposed with other cadences 2 Perfect and imperfect cadences

Recordings

Examples of perfect cadences from Haydn,
Gilbert and Sullivan, rock and roll
 	
1 Cadence recognition
  (a)–(b) *Swing Low, Sweet Chariot*
  (c)   Corelli: Sonata in F, op.5 no.10,
            Sarabanda bars 1–8
  (d)   Rock cadence 2 (JN)
  (e)   Folk dance
  (f)   Dvořák: *American String Quartet,*
            third movement bars 1–8
 	
2   Jeremiah Clarke: *The Prince of*
            Denmark's March

Answers

1 (a) *Swing Low, Sweet Chariot* (bars 1–4)   (imperfect cadence)
  (b) The same (bars 5–8)   (perfect cadence)
  (c) Corelli: Sarabanda   (perfect cadence)
  (d) Rock cadence 2   (plagal cadence)
  (e) Folk dance   (imperfect cadence)
  (f) Dvořák: *American Quartet*   (perfect cadence)

2   *The Prince of Denmark's March*
    line 1   imperfect cadence
    line 2   perfect cadence
    line 4   imperfect cadence
    line 5   imperfect cadence
    line 7   imperfect cadence
    line 8   imperfect cadence (or perfect cadence in A)
    line 10 perfect cadence

Related listening

Khachaturian: Gayane, 'Sabre Dance' (for one-chord tune with alternating bass, later transposed up a minor 3rd, and also repeated notes)
'Holding back the years' from *Picture Book*: Simply Red (for revolving two-chord accompaniment)
'Take a chance on me' from *Abba's Greatest Hits* (for V and I *a capella*)
Mozart: Symphony no. 39 in E♭ third movement (trio) (for imperfect and perfect cadences)
'I'm reviewing the situation' from *Oliver!*: Lionel Bart (for imperfect and perfect cadences)
Walton: *Façade*, 'Jodelling song' (for piece based entirely on I and V with clear perfect cadence at end)

Groups and families 2

<table>
<tr><td>

Featured elements

1 String quartet
   textures
   conversation
   dynamics

2 Brass quintet
   imitation
   melodic extension
   $\frac{5}{4}$ time
   texture

3 Wind quintet
   exchange of motifs
   repeated notes
   texture and contrast
   melodic extension

</td><td>

Recordings

1 Mozart: String Quartet in B♭ K 458, fourth movement bars 1–46

2 Victor Ewald: Symphony for five-part brass choir, op.5, second movement, third section

3 Geoffrey Winters: *Contrasts on a Theme from Liszt*, op. 54, fourth movement

</td></tr>
</table>

Answers

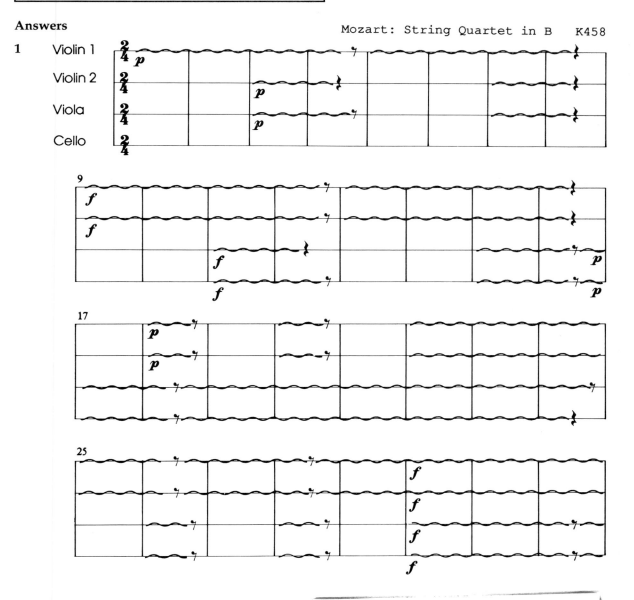

Mozart: String Quartet in B   K458

Light and shade 2

2 (a) In the extract from the Ewald symphony the 1st trumpet plays mostly chord notes.

   (b) The first trumpet extends the tune by first repeating it (a 3rd) higher (in sequence), before bringing it to a high-pitched climax followed by a drooping figure which occurs three times.

   (c) The texture becomes simpler with long held notes on two instruments and quavers on two others. The first trumpet is silent after one bar of semiquavers.

   (d) In the last two bars, which are introduced by the reappearance of the first trumpet, the cadence chords are played three times, with the last pair being stretched out (augmented). They are melodically related to the drooping figure.

3 The middle section of the extract from Geoffrey Winters' *Contrasts* extends the bassoon idea accompanied at first with downward, semiquaver figures on the clarinet. Then the horn enters with a quaver figure which becomes more insistent as it grows to a climax. The texture of the middle section, except for a brief moment at the climax, is in two parts only.

Related listening

'Yesterday' from *Help*: The Beatles (string quartet as backing)
Bartók: String Quartet no. 5, scherzo (for textural contrast)
Malcolm Arnold: Brass Quintet (for brilliant brass writing)
Malcolm Arnold: *Three Shanties* for wind quintet (for entertaining wind writing)
Mozart: any wind divertimenti
Also recordings of The Fairer Sax (or other saxophone group) for similar examples of unified instrumental timbre

Light and shade 2

Featured elements
1 Legato and staccato
2 Comparison of articulation

3 Identification of errors of:
   pitch
   rhythm
   articulation

Recordings

Illustration of legato and staccato from Mozart: String Quartet in G K 387, fourth movement

1 (a)–(b) Victor Ewald: Symphony for five-part brass choir
    (c) Susato: Ronde
    (d) Beethoven: Symphony no. 3, third movement, trio

2 Three single bar fragments (×2)

3 Recorder melody (GW) (×2)

3 As printed in student's book

As played on recording

Related listening

Chopin: *Studies*, op. 25 no. 4 in A minor (for staccato and legato), and no. 9 in G♭ major (for ♩♩♩♩ phrasing)
Walton: *Façade*, 'Jodelling song' (for clear differentiation between staccato motifs and legato phrases)
Debussy: *Preludes* book 2, 'General Lavine' (for staccato triads and clearly articulated melody)

Listening test 2A

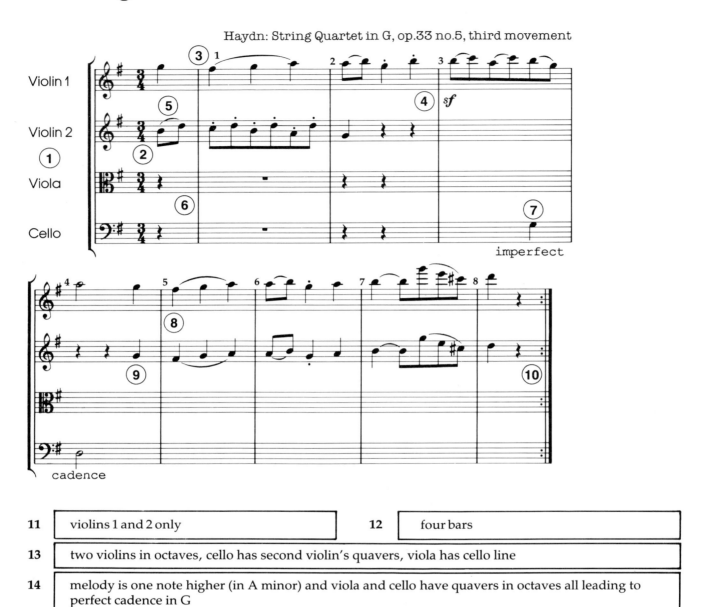

Haydn: String Quartet in G, op.33 no.5, third movement

imperfect

cadence

11	violins 1 and 2 only	12	four bars

13	two violins in octaves, cello has second violin's quavers, viola has cello line

14	melody is one note higher (in A minor) and viola and cello have quavers in octaves all leading to perfect cadence in G

15	a string quartet	16	Haydn

Listening test 2B

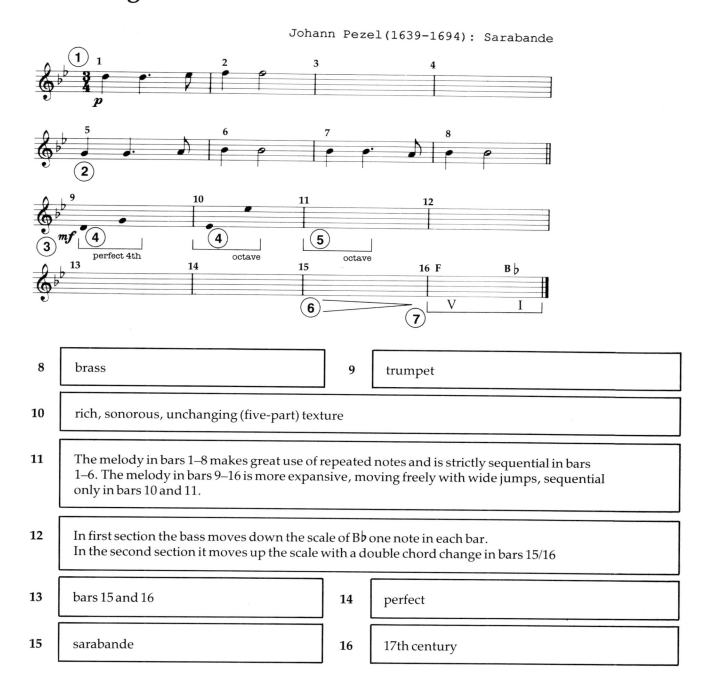

Johann Pezel (1639–1694): Sarabande

| 8 | brass | 9 | trumpet |

| 10 | rich, sonorous, unchanging (five-part) texture |

| 11 | The melody in bars 1–8 makes great use of repeated notes and is strictly sequential in bars 1–6. The melody in bars 9–16 is more expansive, moving freely with wide jumps, sequential only in bars 10 and 11. |

| 12 | In first section the bass moves down the scale of B♭ one note in each bar. In the second section it moves up the scale with a double chord change in bars 15/16 |

| 13 | bars 15 and 16 | 14 | perfect |

| 15 | sarabande | 16 | 17th century |

Listening test 1A

Listening test 1B

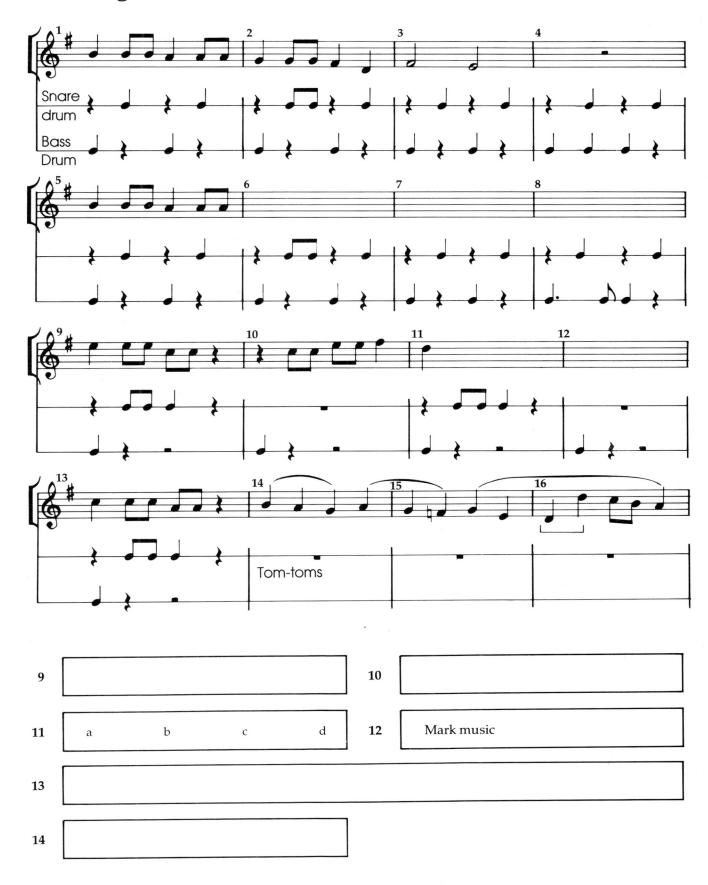

Listening test 2A

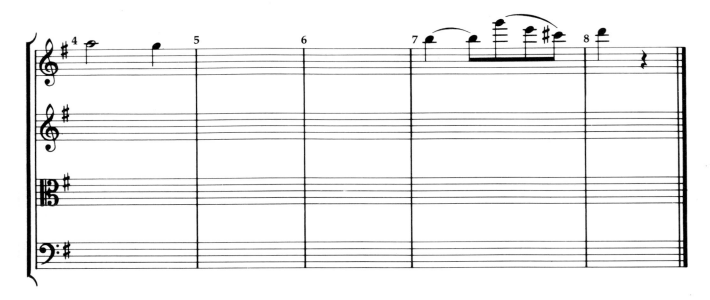

Listening test 2B

Listening test 3A

Listening test 3B

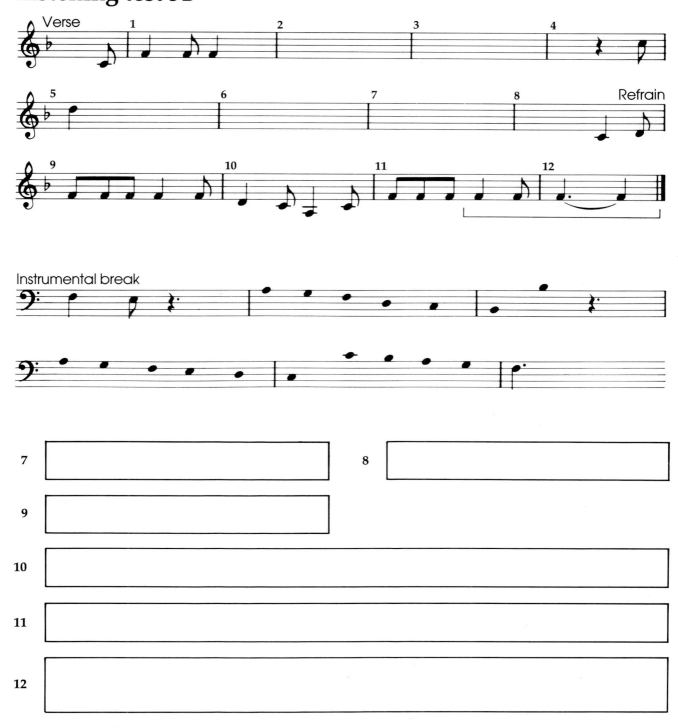

Listening test 4A

Listening test 4B

2a [ ]

b [ ]

c [ ]

d [ ]

e [ ]

f [𝄢]

3 [ ]

Level 3

Beats and bars 3

<table>
<tr><td>

Featured elements

1   $\frac{6}{8}$ ♩.   ♩♪   and   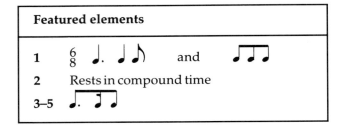

2   Rests in compound time

3–5   ♩.   ♩ ♩

</td><td>

Recordings

1   $\frac{6}{8}$ rhythms (×2)

2   $\frac{6}{8}$ rhythm in 2 parts (×2)

3   *Blow the Man Down, Bullies*

4   Melodic extracts from:
    (a) Bizet: *Carmen*, Guard music
    (b) Wagner: *Die Walküre*

5   Haydn: String Quartet in G, op.33 no.5,
    fourth movement bars 1–32

</td></tr>
</table>

Answers

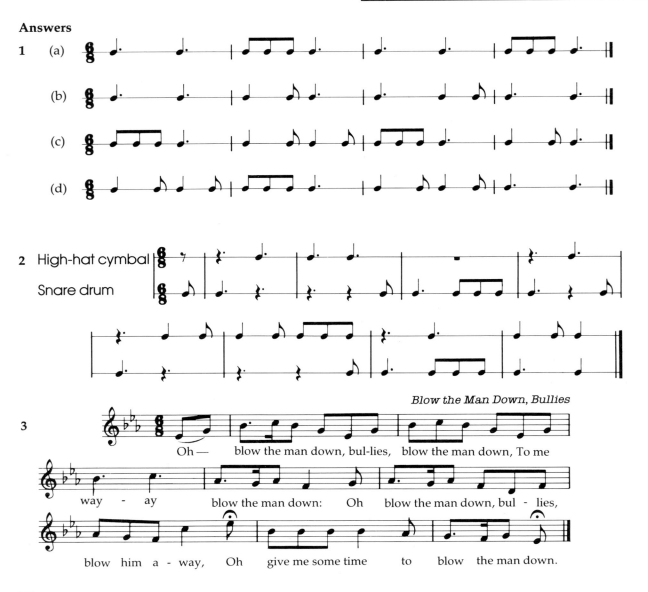

Blow the Man Down, Bullies

Bizet: *Carmen*

4 (a)

Wagner: *Die Walküre*

(b)

5 Illustrative. You might draw attention to the end of the first part which ends on an imperfect cadence, but in the key of E minor, and notice that in the first variation, the first violin ranges widely as it embellishes the melody over the rhythmic and harmonic structure of the theme.

Related listening

Sumer is icumen in and other medieval dance tunes (for basic compound rhythms)
'Bach goes to Limerick' from *Commoner's Crown:* Steeleye Span (for compound rhythms and rests)
Borodin: *Polovtsian Dances,* presto (for fast reiterated long–short rhythm written as ♩ 𝄾 ♩)
Dvořák: *Romance* for violin and orchestra, op.11 (for ♩. ♩♩ prominently in main tune)

Shapes and sizes 3

<table>
<tr><td>

Featured elements

1 $\frac{6}{8}$ melody, slotting melodic fragments into incomplete tune

2–3 melodies with chord shapes, sequences

4 pentatonic melodies

</td><td>

Recordings

1 Russell: *A Life on the Ocean Wave* (for brass quintet, arranged GW)

2 Fiddle tune: *Rattle the Cash*

3 Playford: *Dargason*

4 Dvořák: *American String Quartet,* first movement bars 1–12

</td></tr>
</table>

Answers

Russell: *A Life on the Ocean Wave* (brass quintet arranged GW)

1

Coda

Irish fiddle tune: *Rattle the Cash*

2

Playford: *Dargason*

3

4 (a) The five *different* notes are F, G (once only) A, C and D.
   (b) They are written in the alto clef because they are played by the viola. (As an exercise try rewriting them in treble or bass clefs and note the number of leger lines needed.)
   (c) After the notated extract, the violin repeats the tune and then extends it sequentially.
   (d) The violins have two bars' introduction playing tremolo.

Related listening

Beethoven: Symphony no.6, fifth movement (for chord shape melody in $\frac{6}{8}$)
Mozart: Horn Concerto no.3 in E♭ K 447, third movement (for repeated-note figures and sequences in compound time)
Smetana: *The Bartered Bride,* overture (for pentatonic melody in introduction and elsewhere)
'Buttons and Bows' from the film *Son of Paleface* (pentatonic except for final cadence)
Sailing: Rod Stewart (pentatonic shape with some fourth degree, but no seventh)
In addition, many Negro spirituals are pentatonic

Chords and cadences 3

Featured elements	Recordings
1 Melodies with phrases based on tonic and sub-dominant chords in the key of F. In solfa, soh lah soh	1 Extracts from melodies with soh lah soh. (a) *For He's a Jolly Good Fellow* (b) *Fire Down Below* (c) *One More River* (d) *Oats, Beans and Barley, 0!* (e) *The Rio Grande*
2 Chord of IV in key F Plagal cadence	2 *For He's a Jolly Good Fellow* (instrumental version)
3 Recognition of: perfect cadence imperfect cadence plagal cadence	3 Folk dance: *The Quaker's Wife*

Answers

1 (a) Fire, fire, fire (from *Fire Down Below*)
   (b) And so say all of us (from *For He's a Jolly Good Fellow*)
   (c) Oats, beans and barley, O!
   (d) O Rio (from *The Rio Grande*)
   (e) One more river

Light and shade 3

Featured elements	Recordings
1 *Pizzicato, con sordino* and other special ways of playing string instruments 2 Mutes and brass instruments 3 Woodwind effects	Talk through tape for demonstration 1 Paul Patterson: String Quartet, second movement 2 Geoffrey Winters: *Mutations* for two trumpets, third movement 3 Klaus Huber: *Ein Hauch von Unzeit I*

Answers

1 The three melodic quotations use the same notes with different octave displacements and rhythms. The third example makes use of enharmonic notation for notes like C♯ and D♭ and, more importantly, adds one extra note, a C. This makes it a melody with twelve different notes.

   The downward scale idea in quavers ends the movement, although it is followed by a G and C on the cello, which not only inverts the prominent perfect 5th of the main idea, but also hints at a perfect cadence.

   The changes in dynamic level are of two types. Sudden movements from *p* to *f* plus some passages which grow louder and softer over a number of bars. Both these are illustrated at the end where four bars' *crescendo* is followed by four bars' *diminuendo* and then an unexpected pair of *forte* notes in the bass.

2

3 Illustration of woodwind effects.

Related listening

Bartók: String Quartet no.4, fourth movement (for varied pizzicato)

Britten: *Simple Symphony*, 'Playful pizzicato' (for pizzicato in compound time with chord-note shapes mixed with steps and repeated notes)

Tchaikovsky: Symphony no.4 in F minor, third movement (probably the most famous pizzicato movement, but listen also to the trios for woodwind and then brass)

Listen to any of the *Level 42* album (for slap bass techniques)

Berlioz: *Symphonie Fantastique*, fifth movement (for *col legno* towards climax)

Walton: *Façade* (for considerable use of muted trumpet in 'Tango Pasodoble', 'Tarantella' (compound time) and 'Popular Song')

Black and Tan Fantasy: Duke Ellington (for expressive muted brass)

'Holding back the years' from *Picture Book*: Simply Red (for muted trumpet conversation with vocal)

'Take me to the Mardi Gras' from *Paul Simon's Greatest Hits* (for New Orleans jazz band in brass, and woodwind glissandi and slides)

Khachaturian: *Gayane* 'Sabre Dance' (for glissandi on muted trumpet and trombone as well as on strings)

'Goodbye Stranger' from *Breakfast in America*: Supertramp, and 'Shaft' (film theme) (for comparison of wah-wah pedal effect on guitar with cup mute on brass)

Berio: *Sequenza I* for flute, *Sequenza VII* for oboe (for modified woodwind techniques)

Varèse: *Density 21.5* (for solo flute techniques including key tapping). The title is derived from the metallic density of the platinum flute of Georges Barrère for whom it was written.

Listening test 3A

Carl Stamitz: Trio op.14

8	trio sonata because there are two solo instruments with a continuo

9	flute		10	violin

11	thirds

12	harpsichord and viola da gamba (or cello)

13	(i) *p* instead of *mf* (ii) repeated notes (iii) new rhythmic feature also (iv) change of key to D (v) melodic contour changed

14	(i) near sequence (ii) *piano* repeat of last two bars also effect of minor key in bar 13, and repeated chord progression IV V I

Listening test 3B

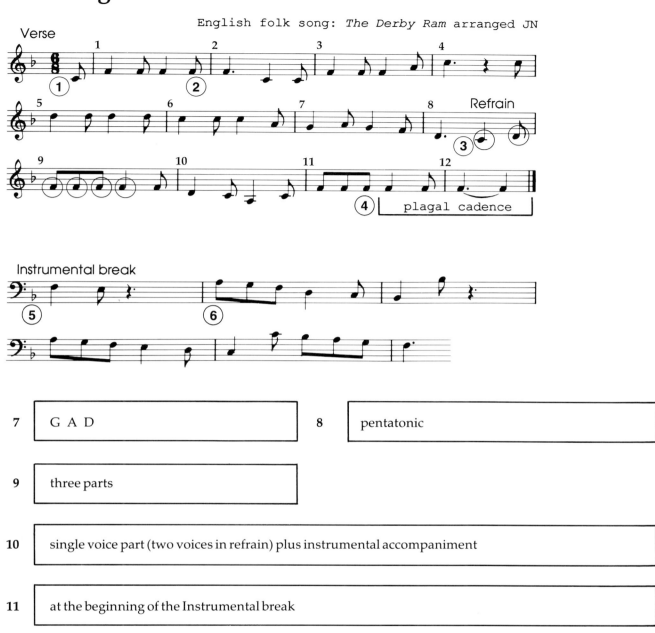

English folk song: *The Derby Ram* arranged JN

| 7 | G A D | 8 | pentatonic |

| 9 | three parts |

| 10 | single voice part (two voices in refrain) plus instrumental accompaniment |

| 11 | at the beginning of the Instrumental break |

| 12 | The final refrain is repeated, it has cadential pause (interrupted cadence) and ends on a bare 5th |

Level 4

Beats and bars 4

Featured elements		Recordings
1–2 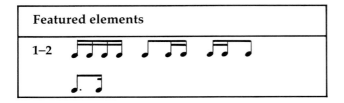		1 No recording
		2 Robert Farnon: *Bandutopia* bars 1–70

Answers

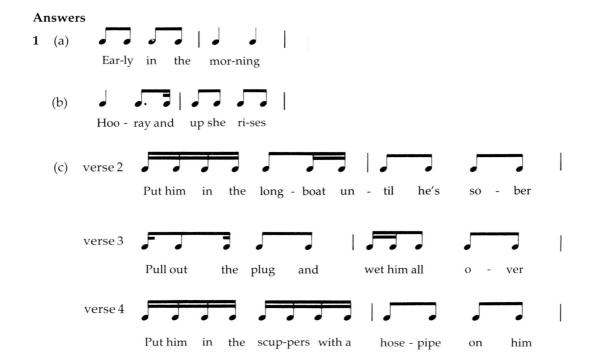

1 (a)
    Ear-ly in the mor-ning

(b)
    Hoo - ray and up she ri-ses

(c) verse 2
    Put him in the long - boat un - til he's so - ber

verse 3
    Pull out the plug and wet him all o - ver

verse 4
    Put him in the scup-pers with a hose - pipe on him

Robert Farnon: *Bandutopia*

2

Introduction on cornets using

C	Um-pa um-pa accompanying idea on horns and basses growing louder and softer

Solo cornet tune

D	Tune on all cornets, played more loudly and extended with more ♩♪♪♩ figures

Sequence based on

A	Jaunty tune on trombones ending with syncopated glissandi

Jaunty tune on cornets and horns

B	[musical notation]

First tune back again an octave lower on euphonium and other instruments

Related listening

'Lessons in love' from *Running in the Family:* Level 42 (for ♪♫ rhythms in chordal bass riff)
Gilbert and Sullivan: *Iolanthe*, 'Entrance and March of the Peers' (for ♪♫ rhythms in chord-tune fanfare)
Kodály: *Háry János*, 'Viennese Musical Clock' (for extensive use of ♫)
Stravinsky *Petrushka*, 'Russian Dance' from 1st tableau (for ♪♫ and ♫♫)
Smetana: *The Bartered Bride*, 'Polka' (for ♫)
Walton: *Façade*, 'Polka' (for ♫♫♪)
Walford Davies: *RAF March Past* (for ♪. ♫♫♫ and ♪♫)

Shapes and sizes 4

Featured elements		**Recordings**	
1–2	Dorian mode	1	No recording
3	Minor keys, harmonic and melodic scales, shapes and intervals	2	Melodic extract from Kodály: *Háry János*, IV bars 5–12 (×2)
		3	No recording
		4	Paganini: *Caprice* for solo violin bars 1–12

Shapes and sizes 4

Answers

Related listening

Bach: Suite in B minor, 'Badinerie' (for ♪♫ in minor chord-shape melody)

Mendelssohn: *Fingal's Cave* Overture (for ♫ in minor with sequence)

Kodály: *Háry János*, 'The Battle and Defeat of Napoleon' (for full enjoyment of modal tune used in exercise 2 – includes trombone glissandi, triplets, trills, ♫ in compound section, and a saxophone solo as well as extensive percussion)

Variations: Andrew Lloyd Webber (for cello and rock group variations on Paganini *Caprice*). Also used for South Bank Show theme music

A few English carols like *God Rest You Merry Gentlemen* and *Down in Yon Forest* (for whole tone melodic movement between keynote and natural seventh)

Chords and cadences 4

<table>
<tr><td>

Featured elements

Chords in minor keys

Whole tone chordal movement between tonic and natural seventh

1 Recognition of chords of I, VII and V$_7$

2 Listening to:
    bass movement
    melodic variation
    instrumental distribution

</td><td>

Recordings

---

1 Folk dance tunes:
   (a) *The Old Grey Cat*
   (b) *Gilderoy*

2 Ibert: *Deux Interludes* no.2, second part of movement

</td></tr>
</table>

Answers

The Old Grey Cat

1 (a)

Gilderoy

(b)

2 Ibert: *Deux Interludes* no.2
   (a) Violin plays off-beat pizzicato in bars 3 and 7.
   (b) Melody is varied with repeated syncopated A.
   (c) Violin joins in third line and plays in thirds from middle of bar 10.
   (d) Violin has flute tune an octave lower when it takes over melodic role.
   (e) Harpsichord plays semiquaver figuration.
   (f) Flute and violin converse.
   (g) Music dies away following short chromatic scales on violin and flute.

Groups and families 4

Related listening

Holiday: Madonna (for side-stepping harmony like A minor, G, F, G, A minor)
Who's that girl?: Madonna (for side-stepping harmony in minor)
'Another girl' from *Help*: The Beatles (for side-stepping harmony)
Chopin: Study in A minor, op.25 no.11 (for ♩ ♫♩ ♩ on chords in minor)
Turpin Hero and *Old Joe Clarke* as well as many Irish fiddle tunes (for easily recognisable melodic shapes based on side-stepping chords like E minor and D)
Note that this may be an appropriate point at which to draw attention to the upward step of chords V and VI as one form of interrupted cadence.

Groups and families 4

Featured elements	Recordings
Vocal range, type and combination (a) Overlaying rhythm above words (b) Recognition of: 　　male, female and mixed voices 　　unison and harmony 　　rhythmic unison 　　chords I, IV and V 2　Recognition of solo, unison and harmony 3　Vocal imitation	1　Gilbert and Sullivan: *The Pirates of Penzance*, Act 1, part of finale. 2　E.M. Bostwick *We Were Gathering up the Roses in the Wild Wood* from 'Songs of Yale' 3　Wilbye: *Adieu Sweet Amaryllis*, bars 1 – 5

Answers

1

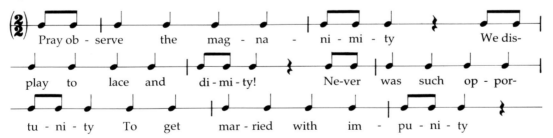

Pray ob - serve the mag - na - ni - mi - ty We dis-
play to lace and di - mi - ty! Ne - ver was such op - por-
tu - ni - ty To get mar - ried with im - pu - ni - ty

Pirates sing first in unison (with major-general)
Girls follow with same melody
When all sing in harmony, rhythm remains the same, with a different melody.
Sopranos hold long note over largely crotchet movement at the words 'Tho' a doctor of divinity' growing into a rich, modulating cadence passage in longer notes.
Orchestral postlude returns to first melody over I I I V7, and then fragments it.over chords I and IV in a reiterated plagal cadence.

2　*We Were Gathering up the Roses in the Wild Wood.*

Solo lines	Unison lines
Oh the look she gave to me	Tiddily-um Oh the look she gave to him Tiddily-um

3

Wilbye: *Adieu Sweet Amaryllis*

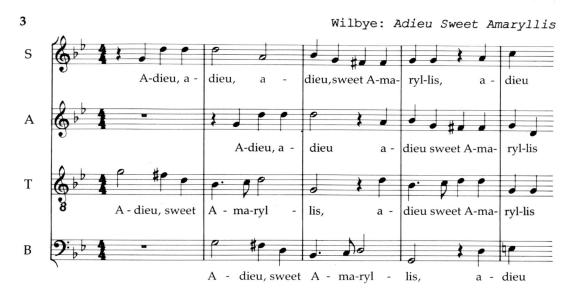

Related listening

Mozart: *The Marriage of Figaro*, Act 1, 'La vendetta' (Now for vengeance) Doctor Bartolo (for basso buffo at its best), and 'Non piu andrai' (Say goodbye now) Figaro (for ♩♪ in famous baritone aria); Act 2, 'Porgi amor' (God of love) Countess (soprano), 'Voi che sapete' (Tell me fair ladies) Cherubino (for soprano in male role), and Finale (for perfection in vocal counterpoint and characterisation)

'For you' from *Welcome to the Cruise:* Judy Tzuke (for multitrack individual voice in modal harmony with string quartet interlude)

'Walking in the air' theme from *The Snowman*: sung by Aled Jones (for illustration of treble voice)

Only you: The Flying Pickets (male voice *a capella* for comparison with barber-shop). Listen also to The King's Singers.

The Boogie Woogie Bugle Boy from Company B: The Andrew Sisters, and more recently Bette Midler (for female close harmony vocals)

'Loves me like a rock' from *Paul Simon's Greatest Hits* (for mixed male and female gospel-style antiphony)

Listen to English and Italian madrigals as well as to vocal music by composers such as Monteverdi, Dowland and Purcell.

Light and shade 4

<table>
<tr><td>Featured elements</td></tr>
</table>

Featured elements

1   Electronic sound processing:
      reverberation (gated)
      double tracking or harmonising
      echo or delay
      sampling

2   Electronic techniques in composition

Recordings

Demonstration talk-through tape

1   *Rock Study Two* (JN)

2   *Malabar Moods* (JN)

Answers

1   [E] [B] [A] [D] [C]

2

zing-tonk motifs	repetitive tapping	chattering cascades	a sustained single note
metallic twirlings	chattering cascades	extended twirlings and zing-tonk motifs	climactic clashes

Related listening

'Don't lose my number' from *No Jacket Required*: Phil Collins (for gated reverb(eration) on drums and repeat echo vocals to accentuate the words 'way' and 'back' on side-stepping modal harmony)

Nineteen: Paul Hardcastle (for sampled, repeated, stuttered verbal segments)

Owner of a lonely heart: Yes (for sampled orchestral stab in introduction)

Stockhausen's Greatest Hits (double LP) (for overview of electronic and other modern techniques)

Varèse: *Integrales* (for the use of 'sound masses'). Although this piece is not electronic, Varèse later experimented with electronic techniques which reflect similar aims in the use of sound as an entity.

Listening test 4A

| 3 | chords change twice in each bar | 4 | bass | 5 | male |

6 | bass instruments have melody like Sergeant's (higher instruments have tarantara motif). Sequential treatment including extension of ♩.♪ rhythm then single-beat notes move to longer notes before repeated chord of C.

7 | higher voices and solo continue tarantara, at first on same note (dominant) but then take up melody which has been started in orchestra. Orchestral bass descends from G to C before being joined by lower voices on alternating bass part. Ends with perfect cadence.

*for information, chords not asked for from this point in question 2

Listening test 4B

S. Johnson: Suite *The Golden West* 'On the trail'

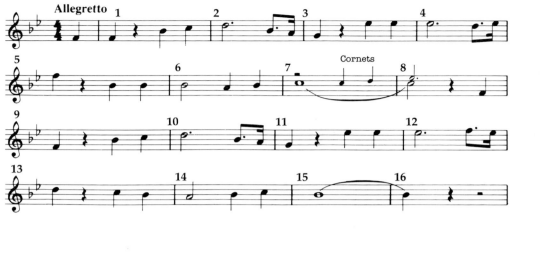

2 (a) | thirds

(b) | an upward scale

(c) | euphoniums and baritone

(d) | repeated notes

(e) | trombones

(f)

3 | catchy rhythms
muted cornets
wood blocks
brushes on the drum